Unnatural

Prayer

By Joe Hamper

www.ChurchSalt.com

Hi, thanks for picking me up!

Wow! You picked up a book on prayer? For some strange reason, not many people do that. Books about end-time events, raising children and having a healthy marriage (or bank account) are usually a lot more popular. But for whatever reason, here we are, and I couldn't be happier about it! Prayer is communication with our Creator and it has more consequence than we will ever know this side of eternity. It changes not just circumstances, but also those who pray. If you have been under the conviction that you need to pray more, and more "properly", I think you grabbed the right book. Another book you should grab right about now is the Bible. You will see a lot of references to Scripture on the following pages and it's always a good idea to check out the context of those references and make sure it says what I say it's saying. This stuff is important! We need to make sure we keep our thoughts and beliefs in-line with God's written Word. So with Bible in hand and our hearts ready to reach out to our Lord in prayer, let's get started. Again, thanks for picking me up!

Contents

INTRODUCTION

Guess what? You just decided to read a book written by a guy who feels extremely unqualified to write it! I guess that's not the way I should introduce this little book, but I wanted to be honest right up front. If you feel as though you don't pray often enough or for the right things in the right way, you aren't alone; I'm with you! In fact, after writing the bulk of this book to be the curriculum for a Sunday School class, it sat on a shelf for years because I couldn't get over the "who am I to teach on prayer?" complex I had developed. But then it hit me, I'm *not* the one teaching on prayer here. All this book is, in essence, is a concentrated look at what the Lord Jesus taught on prayer. Now there's somebody qualified! If we all understood prayer better, if we truly understood what it does, we would no doubt bring ourselves to pray more. So, let's go through this book together and try to learn exactly what our Lord taught about it, shall we? It's my hope that we will all spend more time in prayer after completing it and that prayer will become a consistent part of our lives for the rest of our days, not because we *should* do it, but because we desperately *want* to do it, and because we recognize our need for it It is intended to bring us to a self-examination of our prayer time and the basic foundations of our relationship with the one true God.

As we go, I hope the reasoning behind the title of this book becomes clear. After all, "unnatural prayer" has an odd sound to it, right? The simple fact is that all us humans tend to be self-centered by nature. The cause of this can be traced back to the Garden of Eden where our forefather Adam plunged the entire race into a heritage, a birthright so-to-speak, of sinful desires. With our desires now naturally inclined to ourselves and our own passions, a prayer that focus on our Lord and His will instead of our own can feel very unnatural at times.

But it is this kind of prayer, a prayer in alignment with His will and values, that we are taught to pray and even commanded to pray. And it is only this kind of prayer that God promises to hear and answer. We will learn more of these things as we go, but you might already be getting an idea of why such prayers might at first feel a bit "unnatural."

Since prayer is only half of our conversation with God we are going to try to learn about it by examining the other half (Scripture) more than by using human reasoning. It seems to me that if we want to know how to speak to God, we should first listen to what He's already said to us. I know there's been a lot of talk in the last few years that prayer also includes us listening while He talks back, but where did that idea come from? Nowhere in Scripture are we instructed to do this. To say that the "still small voice" that one believer (Elijah) heard one time in history is how our Lord regularly speaks to all believers is an incredible leap (if not a twisting) from what we see on the pages of the Bible.[1] But God has indeed spoken, and if you own a Bible then you have a copy of what the most all-knowing and all-powerful being in the universe has to say right in your hands! So listen to what He says there and speak back to Him in prayer. That's how conversations work, right? Both sides speak. So on that note, let's start by taking a look at this puzzling statement found in the book of Isaiah:

"And He saw that there was no man, <u>and wondered that there was no intercessor</u>" *Isaiah 59:16*[2]

---

[1] Read 1 Kings 18 & 19 to see entire story of Elijah in context. It is a historical event, not a teaching of how or why we are to communicate with God.

[2] Isaiah 59 is an amazing chapter teaching the sinfulness of men as well as the justice & righteousness of the God who redeems those unworthy. Check it out!

This verse was written at a time when judgment was looming over Isaiah's people and wickedness was everywhere, yet nobody was earnestly seeking God in prayer for deliverance. It's an amazing verse, if you stop to think about it. What could possibly make the all-knowing God of Heaven marvel in wonder? Perhaps the devoted love that some great man shows toward his Lord? No. Or maybe what amazes Him is a self-sacrificing deed that cost some dear saint her life, a deed done for the love of her family? Again, no. The thing we see our Lord wondering over is that nobody is praying. He "wondered", in Hebrew the word is "shâmêm" – it means the Lord was stunned, amazed and in wonderment. Why…how…could He be in wonder over this? It's because He sees the truth of reality (all of reality, even the aspects invisible to us) and knows what prayer is and what it does. He marvels over the lack of desire found in mankind when it comes to prayer. This alone should stir our curiosity and drive us to learn more about prayer! If the all-knowing and all-powerful Lord marvels over our lack of prayer, it's a pretty sure sign that there might be more to it than we think.

As you go, you will notice footnotes at the bottom of many of the pages.[1] These are to help the serious reader verify if what is being discussed is true. Check em' out! You will also come across discussion questions every few pages. These are for group use if you are reading it with others, but if you're not, read these questions yourself and think them through. Feel free to write the answers in the lines provided. In fact, go ahead and underline, comment or earmark this book until it falls apart! It's meant to be used. At the very back of the book you'll find the appendix where there's a small collection of short articles on various topics that are helpful to a follower of Christ. They're short, to the point, and quite helpful.

---

[1] Like this one!

Now that you know what this little book is about, will you keep reading? It doesn't matter if you became a Christian twenty years ago or just twenty minutes ago, learning more about how to follow the Lord Jesus Christ is always time well spent. So, let's begin…

Note:

As you read you will see boxes like the ones below, each one contains some valuable information:

Remember:
These are "Remember" boxes. They are a summary of that chapter's main point. If you remember nothing else, remember these!

Tech Tip!

Boxes that look like this are technical tips. These are tools you can put in your "tool box". They're practical tips that help you apply what you have been learning. Try them out, they help!

Chapter 1

Prayer - What is it?

I'm sure most of us understand the basics of what prayer is. It's an activity that Christians and folks of almost every religion have been doing since the beginning, and so most of us are somewhat familiar with it. It's talking to God, right? In an effort to pin down the definition a little more precisely, I looked into some of the wording used in Scripture and also read how some of the great saints of old defined it. What came out of the blender was this:

Prayer is humbly turning to God to talk with Him, and it's one of the primary and most natural exercises of true faith.

You may be asking yourself why I didn't simply stick with "talking to God". Well, because after a little bit of study it was obvious that true prayer has a few defining characteristic that should be understood. On the next page is a brief explanation of why I chose some of the words I did in my definition of prayer. Let's take a look:

> **"Humbly"** – True prayer is done in a spirit of humility. In fact, the act of praying naturally carries humility at its heart. It is the admittedly smaller creature reaching out to a much greater being, the one who is his or her maker.

"Turning" – It's taking time to turn from other people and activities to face the Lord directly (spiritually speaking). There is an element of intentional focus in biblical prayer.

"Talking" – In Scripture, prayer isn't some mystical, emotional experience. It isn't "soaking" in a mystical presence but is instead clear, intelligent speech (spoken or unspoken) aimed toward the Lord.

"Natural" – It's one of the most natural activities for those who've been given spiritual life. One who recognizes their sin, their savior and the great power and love of the Lord they serve will naturally call out in prayer the same way a baby naturally gasps for air after being born.

"True Faith" – Many people profess Christianity, but if they don't pray it can hardly be said they actually have true faith. Who could be truly saved from sin and death and now living a life devoted to their Master without turning to regularly talk to Him? Good deeds and religious exercises can be done for many different reasons but true faith usually results in the habit of private prayer.

We see many different types of prayer in Scripture. The long, theologically rich prayers found in Paul's letters, the fast off-the-cuff prayer of Nehemiah 2, and, of course, the prayer of Jesus in John 17 that was spoken through blood, sweat and tears. Those truly redeemed by God pray, and true prayer cannot be faked.

As a Pharisee[1], Saul of Tarsus undoubtedly said many prayers, but when he began to offer up a true and genuine prayer, our Lord gave *that* prayer as proof of genuine salvation to the questioning Ananias.[2] Why? Because true prayer flows from a relationship, an intimacy, with God.[3] Do couples who are in the covenant of marriage ignore each other except at formal, public occasions? Of course not! They speak in private far more often than they do in public, and it's the same way with those who have become God's people. Professing Christians of all sorts can fake a lot of things: preaching, teaching, giving, even difficult trips and projects, all with the intention of showing to themselves and others that they are Christian. But private prayer is seen by no-one. It receives no applause and shows nothing to the world. Not all prayer is private, but all those who truly pray do it privately as well as publicly. You, dear Christian, may not have anywhere near the spiritual understanding and passion of the great saints of old. But if you are truly saved, then I'm confident you have offered sincere and true prayers already and would like to now learn more about it.

Now that we have a basic understanding of what we mean when we use the word "prayer", let's have some more discussion before we continue…

---

[1] Pharisee – Ancient Jewish group that was fanatical in following religious laws and traditions as a way to earn righteousness before God.

[2] Acts 9:11

[3] Scripture also states that God doesn't hear (heed) the prayers of the wicked. See Isaiah 59:2, Psalm 66:18 Proverbs 15:29

Tech Tip!

If you are just starting the habit of a daily prayer time (or trying to re-start it), keep at it! When first starting it can be difficult to verbalize our thoughts, concerns, thanks and requests. The first day will be the toughest, but each day it will get a little easier until the time comes when you are drawn to pray out of your heart's spiritual need to commune with its maker. So keep at it! The flesh wars against the spirit, and sometimes raw determination is needed to get us through the tough spells![1]

Discussion:

1) In your opinion, is there one "correct" way to pray, or does each person have their own correct way?

____

____

____

____

2) God is all knowing, yet we see in Scripture[2] that He wonders at those who don't pray. Does this surprise you? Do you think He has ever marveled over your lack of prayer?

____

____

____

[1] Galatians 5:17

[2] Isaiah 59:16

Discussion *(continued)*:

3) Noted theologian and author Graeme Goldsworthy said this about prayer:

   "Most of us have heard sermons, convention talks or Bible studies that seem to imply or focus on our defective practices of prayer including how undisciplined we are, how lazy, and how lacking in resolve. The effect is to make us feel both guilt and discouragement. A terrible legalism seems to surround the subject of prayer."[1]

   Has this been your experience in past studies on prayer? How much of your motivation in prayer is driven by guilt?

   ____

   ____

   ____

   ____

4) Is a prayer that is motivated by affection for God the same as one that is brought about by a sense of guilt?

   ____

   ____

   ____

   ____

[1] "A Biblical-Theological Perspective on Prayer" by Graeme Goldsworthy is available for free download at *Monergism.com*

Chapter 2

Approaching HIM

In my opinion, it's a good idea pause for a moment and consider the One we are approaching before we go rushing in. Just who is this God we are coming before? What is He like? Every conversation we have is greatly influenced by who we are talking to, right? For example, we talk to our spouse very differently than we talk to the police officer who pulled us over for speeding. We would never talk to our boss with the same tone we use with a small child. Likewise, we must consider who it is we are approaching (and the tone we use) when we come to the throne of God, the Lord of Heaven's Armies, the One who is Faithful and True.

The first and most amazing thing that comes to mind when considering our approach to the Holy God is that we can approach Him at all! That is, the *believer* can approach the throne and be heard. The Bible states in multiple places that the Lord does not hear the prayers of those who are not called by His name.[1] When we think of the multitude of sins we have committed and how many times we have recklessly broken God's law it should bring us fear and amazement that He even listens to our voice.[2] On our own merit, we simply don't deserve to be heard; we deserve His eternal wrath, not His loving ear.

---

[1] Sound strange? Check it out for yourself! See John 9:31, Isaiah 59:2 & Psalm 66:18

[2] A summary of God's law can be found in Exodus 20

When approaching Him, we must remember the reason that we're even able to do this thing. To remind ourselves, let's look in the book of Hebrews:

[19] And so, dear brothers and sisters, we can boldly enter heaven's Most Holy Place because of the blood of Jesus.[20] By his death, Jesus opened a new and life-giving way through the curtain into the Most Holy Place.[21] And since we have a great High Priest who rules over God's house,[22] let us go right into the presence of God with sincere hearts fully trusting him. For our guilty consciences have been sprinkled with Christ's blood to make us clean, and our bodies have been washed with pure water. *- Hebrews 10:19-22*

Wow! Our approach, our very ability to be heard by God, was made possible by the shedding of *divine* blood. Take a moment to think about that – divine blood! The sinless Son of God, God in the flesh, had to die for us so we could even be heard. Surely this brings about a sense of humility and awe, does it not? We also see here the phrase "fully trusting him." Another translation uses the term "full assurance of faith" here.[1] What is this trust and faith mentioned here? Faith in what? The writer is speaking of faith in the complete and sufficient sacrifice of the Savior on his behalf. Faith that His death paid for our sins and that He is faithful to His Word when He promised to save us. It is a faith in His Word, character, mercy and goodness. It is a complete abandonment of any faith we might have in ourselves and our own efforts to somehow "clean up" so as to bring about a right-standing before God through our own feeble efforts and deeds that we call "good".

---

[1] "let us draw near with a true hear in full assurance of faith" – ESV (English Standard Version)

This passage makes one thing very clear: ***All*** who approach God must do so through belief and trust that the blood of Jesus Christ is what makes us right with God and able to approach the Holy Throne.[1] This isn't a new idea. If you're familiar with the descriptions of the temple in the Old Testament you may remember that the mercy seat was located behind the curtain in the Holy of Holies. According to God's law, this area couldn't be approached without blood.[2] Do you also remember how the mercy seat was positioned directly on top of the box containing the law?[3] This is the very picture of Christ's work, isn't it? Mercy hasn't replaced the law, but through the shedding of blood has fulfilled it and so is now in the superior position. And in the same way the law was kept in the Ark of the Covenant, it is now being kept in the hearts of new covenant believers.[4]

The point is this: The one approaching the Mercy Seat would have had an extremely vivid reminder of his sin and guilt (by looking at the law) and his need for atonement (the sprinkled blood received before entering). The people of Israel could indeed approach and ask for mercy through their representative the priest, but not without understanding their guilt and who it was they were approaching. Modern day followers of Christ are part of the true Israel and in the same position, even though we are under the new covenant.[5] With these things in mind, we should take great pains not to take our ability to approach the Lord in a casual manner.

---

[1] Ephesians 2:18

[2] Hebrews 9 and 10 give good explanation of the old covenant approach to the mercy seat.

[3] Exodus 25:21

[4] Jeremiah 31:33

[5] Romans 9:6-8 The true Israel is those who believe the promise (gospel).

Let's now take a moment to think of whose blood has been sprinkled upon us and who it is we are approaching. To do this we'll read the account of someone who approached the Throne and wrote about the experience. In ancient Israel, the Lord hand-picked Isaiah to be His spokesperson and representative on Earth during some of that nation's most troubling days. He was quite possibly the most righteous man on Earth at the time. Let's take a quick look at his experience when he was brought before the God of Heaven:

[1] In the year that King Uzziah died I saw the Lord sitting upon a throne, high and lifted up; and the train of his robe filled the temple. [2] Above him stood the seraphim. Each had six wings: with two he covered his face, and with two he covered his feet, and with two he flew. [3] And one called to another and said: "Holy, holy, holy is the LORD of hosts; the whole earth is full of his glory!" [4] And the foundations of the thresholds shook at the voice of him who called, and the house was filled with smoke. [5] And I said: "Woe is me! For I am lost; for I am a man of unclean lips, and I dwell in the midst of a people of unclean lips; for my eyes have seen the King, the LORD of hosts!" *- Isaiah 6:1-5*

Here we see a righteous man of God approach the throne and ...collapse! He thought he was doomed! He recognizes his speech (his lips) testified to the evil of his heart and the evil in the hearts of his people (a person's speech revealing the state of his heart is a biblical teaching[1]). This was a man who would blush scarlet red to even think of the sins that folks nowadays indulge in without any concern whatsoever and yet he is in terror when he sees the purity, glory and power of the Lord on His Throne. Another interesting thing to note in this passage is that Isaiah approached the Lord... and lived!

---

[1] Matthew 15:18

How can this be since it's stated in Exodus that no man may see the face of God the Father and live?[1] The answer is found in the New Testament book of John where we learn that the One on the throne in front of Isaiah is none other than Jesus Christ Himself![2] God the Son seated upon the throne makes Isaiah come apart, torn with shock and despair and yet God the Father, the one to whom we pray, is of such radiance and glory that we will die if we look upon Him. This is who we are approaching! God the Father – The Unapproachable – and yet, approach we do because Christ made it possible by sprinkling us with His blood.

So as we prepare to humbly turn and face the Lord in prayer, we must never forget who our Lord is and what He is like.[3] He loves us, He has adopted us, He has made a way that we might approach, He calls us sons and daughters, but none of these things change who God really is and what He is like. He is holy, majestic and powerful! It seems to be the modern teaching that we should approach God the same way we might approach an old friend we bump into at the local diner. But this casual attitude toward God is found nowhere in Scripture! Every single time someone has a "God encounter" that person ends up on the ground terrified. They become a quivering puddle of jelly before the majesty and power of the Lord of Hosts. Even John, the humble and tender-hearted disciple who leaned back on Jesus at the last Passover meal was struck down "like one dead" when he saw Jesus in His current state.[4] So when coming to the Lord in prayer, don't forget to whom you are speaking! We are to be afraid, yet bold. Trembling in awe, and yet familiar with Him. Acutely aware of His justice and purity, yet humbled by His grace.

---

[1] Exodus 33:20

[2] John 12:41

[3] What God is like, His qualities are referred to as the "attributes of God"

[4] Revelation 1:17

Remember:
In approaching the Lord, remember who you are and what you have done as well as who He is, and what He has done so that you might be heard!!

Tech Tip!

As you pray, remember that prayer is like using a telephone to talk to somebody else. In the same way you might call a powerful and influential friend who then decides what to do in regards to your conversation, so also you are calling your God. It's been said that there is great power in prayer, but technically speaking, this is completely false! The one with temple-shaking power is the Lord, not the phone you use to call Him. It's good to remember this distinction so we don't deceive ourselves into thinking that it's our prayers that are accomplishing change. They aren't. All the credit goes to our wonderful God and Savior!

Discussion:

1) Have you ever seen an approach to prayer you felt was wrong? When thinking of all the prayers you thought were somehow wrong, can you think of any traits they have in common?

____

____

____

____

Discussion (continued):

2) Is a casual approach of the Lord disrespectful or is it simply coming from familiarity and love? Is it sinful?[1]

    ____

    ____

    ____

    ____

3) Many modern teachers say we should approach God not just boldly, but with prayers that could be called "audacious". In Scripture, do you know of any prayers that come from a sense of entitlement or a demand that God fill the desires of a person's heart? What common traits do you see in most Biblical prayers?

    ____

    ____

    ____

    ____

[1] 2 Samuel 6:5-7

Chapter 3

The Lesson Begins

So now we know what prayer is as well as a little bit about approaching the throne. Now what? Should we just pray however we want or should we use some type of format in our prayer? Is there such a thing as praying "correctly"? Some have a legalistic view of prayer, viewing it as a mandatory chore or formula more than as a conversation. In fact, even the discussion of how to pray somehow carries an air of legalism along with it, for we automatically think of "right ways" and "wrong ways" in our minds.

But what do we see in Scripture? One thing we see is men and women of God crying out to Him in different ways with great emotion, being driven along by the passion of their hearts as they were in various trials and circumstances. On the other hand, we also see that the disciples asked Jesus for a "how-to" lesson on prayer, and got one! I think it's clear when looking at the prayers in the Bible that there is no specifically mandated formula and the child of God should feel free to call out in prayer at any time. I think it equally obvious that true believers approach their Lord daily in prayer about the basic issues of life. It's this daily prayer that Jesus teaches His disciples, and a careful study of it reveals much about all prayer and can even help us to pray naturally and more often.

So in our quest to learn to pray, it's to this lesson we will go. After all, who better to teach prayer than the Son of God? The "Lord's Prayer" as it is usually called (although some call it the "Disciple's Prayer") can be found in Matthew chapter six:

"And when you pray, do not heap up empty phrases as the Gentiles do, for they think that they will be heard for their many words. [8] Do not be like them, for your Father knows what you need before you ask him. [9] Pray then like this: "Our Father in heaven, hallowed be your name. [10] Your kingdom come, your will be done, on earth as it is in heaven. [11] Give us this day our daily bread, [12] and forgive us our debts, as we also have forgiven our debtors. [13] And lead us not into temptation, but deliver us from evil. *For yours is the kingdom and the power and the glory forever. Amen - Matthew 6:7-13*

To understand this divine lesson on how to pray, we need to break it up and examine it piece-by-piece. Let's take a look at the very beginning of the lesson found in verse seven:

"And when you pray..."

The first thing to notice here is the assumption "when you pray". It doesn't say "if" you pray. Our Lord is assuming that His true followers will and do pray. When a person is converted, they're adopted into the family of God. Here on Earth, don't the children of a good man enjoy spending time and talking with their father? Of course they do! How much more those of us who have been adopted[1] by the perfect Father of all creation? And adoption into His family isn't the only reason it's natural to pray. Those who are redeemed remember their condemnation before the Great Court and the price that was paid so that they might go free.

---

[1] Galatians 4:7

That memory is enough in itself to drive the truly redeemed to their knees in praise and thanksgiving! Indeed, it's the lack of giving God thanks that is one of the things that proves someone is lost[1]. Let's return to verse 7 and read on:

v7 "do not heap up empty phrases as the Gentiles do, for they think that they will be heard for their many words."

Here we see the Christian is not to chant or practice repetitions like the monks of old and eastern religions teach. Sadly, there is a movement today that encourages Christians to take up some of the practices of the "monastic fathers" with the belief that they bring us closer to God.[2] If one does a little research, it doesn't take long to find that these "monastic fathers" were actually apostates and false teachers who thought that by so-called spiritual practices (repetitive chanting, depriving themselves of comforts, mystic meditation) they could somehow bring themselves into right-standing with God and draw closer to Him in a mystical way. Most of them were an off-shoot of the Roman Catholic Church who at the Council of Trent declared in extremely plain language that they consider a professing believer to be eternally damned to Hell if they believe salvation comes from the life and death of Jesus Christ alone.[3] It was (and is) their belief that salvation comes through both Christ's sacrifice and the believer shaping up and doing good deeds.[4] In other words, they held that the death of Christ wasn't enough to save you and you need to do some of the saving work yourself.

---

[1] Romans 1:21 More on thanksgiving and praise in Chapter 6

[2] Taught under the name "contemplative prayer".

[3] "Anathema" is the word used in the council decrees of those who trust in Jesus alone to pay for sins aside from good works. It means eternally damned.

[4] See Council of Trent Canons 9, 12, 14, 23, 24,30, and 33 - all of which are still in effect today.

In simple language, the practices of these "spiritual fathers" and mystics are simply attempts to ascend to God without relying on Christ's sacrifice alone. In our modern day, they may sound like more spiritual or enlightened ways of worship but in reality they're just a different twist on the age-old heresy by teaching that good religious works lead to a relationship with God. This type of thing is soundly condemned in many places[1], and the monastic style of repetitive prayer is specifically condemned by our Lord Himself here in this passage.

Another way that a person might heap up "empty phrases" is to indulge in long, wordy prayers. I'm sure you have heard them, and maybe even been intimidated by them. These are prayers specifically voiced with the intention of sounding good. They value eloquence over sincerity, and the use of theological terms is often thought to be of high value. Prayers done for the sake of appearance aren't true prayers at all, but are vain exercises in pride. At their heart, empty phrases are empty because they lack humility and sincerity. Whether they take the form of chants, daily prayers said out of habit with little thought to their meaning, or long windy prayers designed to impress, they all have a common: self-centered insincerity. True prayer is not to be this way. Ironically, this model prayer Jesus gives us here has become to many the very thing that Jesus warns against. Countless people recite the "Lord's Prayer" every day as a religious exercise with no sincerity whatsoever. They have turned it into a vain repetition rather than a guideline for their true and heartfelt prayers.

---

[1] See Ephesians 2:8-9, Romans 3:20-24 and Romans 4:20-25

Having said this, please don't misunderstand the meaning behind the phrase "vain repetitions". Just as Jacob wrestled with the angel[1] for a lengthy time we too are told to wrestle with God in prayer.[2] We are to persevere.[3] It is vain repetition that is condemned here, not repetition itself. There is a difference between repeated visits to the throne of God begging Him for action and an empty, formal, religious prayer ritual. There is no value in a prayer that is offered repeatedly out of tradition in the hopes of earning favor as a return for a faithful religious practice. Nor is there any value in using chants or other mind-emptying techniques in an attempt to usher in ecstatic and/or emotional experiences. Let's now look at verse 8 next which reminds us of God's omniscience:

v8 "Do not be like them, for your Father knows what you need before you ask him."

It's amazing how often this fact is neglected in the study of prayer. God knows your needs *before* you ask. He's all-knowing, so whatever is being accomplished during prayer time the one thing we can be sure of that *isn't* happening is this: we aren't educating God on a particular topic. He knows already. In fact, He knew about your current situation before you did! He even knows about the needs you have that you're unaware of yourself. And now we must ask ourselves a very logical and practical question; if God is all-knowing and all-powerful, why do we need to pray in the first place? This is a subject that really needs a lot of time to address thoroughly, but here we will just take a quick fly-by look at Scripture to get four basic answers:

---

[1] Jacob 32:22-30

[2] Romans 15:30, Luke 18:1-8

[3] Luke 18:1-7

Unloading – (1 Peter 5:7) Prayer is an unloading. We unburden ourselves when we cast all our cares on Him, trusting our Lord in faith to do what is best in His eyes. It is the practical result of genuine worship and trust. It's an acting out of our internal faith and it helps that faith (and an accompanying peace) to grow.

Natural – (Acts 9:11) Prayer is natural, and is even given as a sign of true salvation. It's a one-on-one talk with the God who lives and loves. Without this interaction and relationship Christianity is simply an academic exercise or social tradition. For us to ask "why pray?" is similar to a man asking why he should talk with his wife. It's an evidence of true devotion, love and relationship.

Alignment – (Philippians 2:13) God uses many things to change a person's desires and world view, with prayer being one of the primary ways He does this. Prayer is one way our Lord brings us into alignment with His plans, desires and priorities. It's used to separate us from sin and sinful desires and bring us to Him. I refer to it as His "alignment process".

Obedience - (Matthew 6:7-8) It is God's will we pray. This is reason enough, even if we don't understand the logic of it. In this passage, notice that at the same time He assumes we'll pray He also commands us to pray. Weird, huh? Part of calling Him "Lord" is to do what He says, and He commands us to pray.

For now, let's take these reasons and move on, acknowledging that our sovereign Lord does indeed know all, have all power, and yet still commands and expects us to pray. Accepting this, we can now start looking at the heart of the model prayer that Jesus handed down. Let's look at verse nine:

v9 Pray then like this: "Our Father in heaven, hallowed be your name.

Jesus begins by saying, "Pray Like this". Notice He didn't command the use of exact words that we are to memorize and recite but instead tells us that we should pray "like" this; a reference to the style, format and priorities of the prayer.[1] This is the reason that this has been called the "model prayer" by so many godly teachers over the years. To recite the Lord's Prayer as a religious exercise is not only to misunderstand its' purpose, but it also completely misses the heart of God. Our Lord gives this as a model in which might sincerely channel our needs and passions along in such a way so that our prayers accomplish the purpose God. He then begins:

"Our"

Notice this first word , "Our". He doesn't teach us to begin "My Father" but instead uses the plural. While this often slips by unnoticed, I think it deserves a moment of attention. Throughout Scripture, we see that the Christian life is to be lived as a community. The early Church met together, prayed together and lived life together If you read through the book of Acts, it is impossible to come away without understanding what a close-knit community the believers were (and still are today). Further on in the New Testament, the love of believers for each other is even given as a sign of salvation.[2] While we may use this prayer as a model for our private and personal prayer, there is definitely a sense of praying with others in mind. It's the idea of coming to the throne as an individual, but one who is a part of the community of the redeemed. Moving on...

[1] Many translations read "in this manner"

[2] 1 John 3:16-24

“Father”

Here, you the reader might be taking a deep, frustrated breath thinking that we are going to examine every syllable of every word. Please bear with me! I assure you this isn’t the case! But this word “Father” cannot be simply passed over, either. Why? Because it’s the entry, the gateway, for all true prayer. Every time we say this word, we need to pause and ask ourselves this question: Is He my Father? This is what could be called a “go” or “no-go” question, and we must answer it honestly. Scripture makes it clear that only the redeemed, the true Christian, can call the Lord “Father”. The harsh reality is that the non-Christian has no right to this claim.[1] So when approaching our God, examine yourself and your spiritual standing before God. If you have not been adopted into the family of God, the only prayer your lips need to speak is for forgiveness and mercy. Cry out an acknowledgment of your guilt before God (for guilty you are, a quick review of God’s law will convince you of that[2]). Humbly plea for Christ’s payment to be counted on your behalf and transfer the Lordship of your life from self to Him! Put all trust for your salvation in Christ and His work on the Cross. It’s only when you trust Him completely for your rescue and turn from your sin that you will be brought into the family of God and able to call Him “Father” in truthfulness.

If He is indeed your father, pause for a moment and reflect on how this occurred. How did you become a child of God? If you are His, He made you so – it wasn’t your doing! This should be acknowledged with humility and thanksgiving every time you approach in prayer. If I come back to this point a few times in this book, it’s only because it deserves much attention!

---

[1] John 8:44

[2] Exodus 20

All prayer must come through faith in the value of Christ's blood. It's through the blood we enter both His kingdom and family. Any approach through another door is like a thief trying to steal treasures from a house through the back entry. The true son or daughter of God comes through the front door (Christ's blood) of the family home and doesn't come to remove valuables, but to spend time with the loved ones inside. They call the owner of the house "Father" and live peacefully there. The thief at the back door is concerned only with what he can get, what can be removed from the house to benefit him here and now. There are many thieves outside the Father's house trying to get in through many doors they have invented in their own minds. Some are teachers who tell us our words have divine power and that we must make positive confessions in order to receive the peace and treasures inside. Others tell us to boldly demand those things we want and they will be thrown out to us. Still others tell us there is no inside or outside of God's house, and that we will eventually get all treasure simply because the creator is loving. But don't be deceived by such teaching. The Father's true children will enter not as beggars, robbers or bullies but as welcome members of the family who are coming to see the Father out of love. Let's move on...

"Our Father...*in heaven*"

This may sound like a bit of a simplistic point, but it needs to be said. This Father we pray to is the One in Heaven and He is completely different than our earthly father. Those who had fathers who were good men of high morals may think it easier to identify with the righteous Lord as opposed to those who were raised by immoral men or men who didn't fulfill their fatherly duties in any way. That may be true in one regard, but the reality is that our Father in Heaven is so completely different and righteous that there's really no point of comparison with any man.

Remember the passage from Isaiah chapter six we read a few pages ago?[1] The fearsome creatures before the throne crying out day and night were doing something very telling. They weren't proclaiming "loving, loving, loving" though God is indeed loving. Nor did they cry out "righteous, righteous, righteous" which would have also been accurate. The attribute of God that they proclaimed amid the smoke and shaking temple was "Holy, Holy, Holy".[2] This needs to be understood, for it's incredibly important! Our Father in Heaven is Holy. This means He is completely different and "other". He is set apart, with purity and righteousness being at the core of His "otherness". It's commonly understood that the word "Holy" is just another word meaning righteous or good, but that definition doesn't convey the alien otherness that is at the core of this word. Our Father in Heaven is different. He's different from our earthly father, from all earthly fathers, and indeed different from all created beings in all of the universe. Speaking of holiness, our model prayer addresses that very thing next:

"Hallowed be your name"

That is, may your name be kept Holy. May your name and reputation be set apart as pure, undefiled and completely unique. This is the first request we come to in our model prayer, and it isn't a request for our own well-being, but is instead for the purity of God's reputation. God's name is to be kept Holy (separate and pure) and this is to be the top priority in our daily prayer. Are you starting to see why a biblical prayer, a prayer like the one Jesus taught, might feel a bit unnatural? We usually come to our prayer time anxious about our own needs, but instead we are to be focused on our Lord's desires.

---

[1] Isaiah 6:1-5

[2] The word "Holy" has the definition of being set apart, different and sacred with perfection and purity to the very core.

But if the purity of God's name isn't of high priority with you, you need to ask yourself why that is. Is it because you've never reflected on all that He has done and the reputation He deserves? Is it because you don't take time to think about the price He paid to redeem you? Are you redeemed?

While a lack of true conversion may be one reason the holiness of His name is of no concern, the truth is that many soundly saved believers also enter prayer with their own priorities in focus rather than those of their Lord. This is sad but true. Concern for our Savior's Holy name and mission are often never even a thought. This comes from our ungrateful, sinful and self-centered nature that so easily forgets what had to be done to save wretched sinners like ourselves. If this is the case, please allow me to encourage you to spend some quiet time in Scripture to remind yourself just how high the price to save you really was (see footnote below).[1] Try to understand our Lord's priorities and world view and align yourself with them.

When before the throne in prayer, it would be impossible to pray that our Lord's name stays untarnished without reflecting on how we ourselves treat His name and reflect it to others. You see, the professing Christian has an effect on God's reputation whether they want to or not. If a man who is known to attend a Christian church every Sunday and claims to be a Christian is seen throughout the week telling the same jokes as the lost, watching the same television shows as the lost and pursuing the same goals as the lost, doesn't that make Christianity look as though it is no different from the world around it? Doesn't it make the Christian and His Lord appear just as sinful and worldly as others? It does.

---

[1] Isaiah 53 and Luke 23 both describe some of what was endured by Jesus Christ for His people.

Someone who is truly redeemed will naturally strive to live a holy life, a life separate from the world.[1] A life of holiness (separation and purity) is a sign of a true believer. It reflects well on the God who claims that person as a son or daughter and puts the family name in good standing. All things we do should be done for the glory of God.[2] Concern for God's name (reputation) in prayer is just one part of what I call the "alignment process". When someone is saved, our Lord begins to bring about change in their mind, desires and actions. He brings us into alignment with Himself (see Philippians 4:13).[3]

This model prayer is teaching us where our highest priorities should be placed, what concerns we should have, and how we are to be thinking when we come to the Mercy Seat. As we continue to follow this model, our prayers will be moved into agreement with the will of God more and more often so that we can pray with faith, knowing that these prayers will be answered.[4] It will feel unnatural at first, but it's only when we know and understand that we are truly praying according to the will of God that we can be free from doubt and pray with true faith.[5] We also know from Scripture that such confidence in His will comes only through a solid familiarity with the written Word and the renewing of our minds by the Holy Spirit.[6] Here, we must align our desires, actions, and prayers with the fact that God has a jealousy for His name. We will be seeing more of this as we go.

---

[1] Jeremiah 31:33. True believers are always setting themselves apart from the world.

[2] 1 Peter 4 with special attention to verse 11. Also notice the motives for salvation mentioned in Ezekiel 36:22

[3] Also Romans 12:22

[4] Matthew 21:22

[5] 1 John 5:14-15 states that if we ask anything on prayer that is according to His will, He will grant the request. The only way to know His will is to read what He has written.

[6] 2 Peter 1:16-21 shows even Peter, who saw Jesus transfiguration, regarded written Scripture as the sure way to learn of God and His will.

Tech Tip!

R.C. Sproul[1] called the Lord's prayer "A series of pegs that we hang our thoughts upon", meaning it's a model prayer that we are to use verbally as we pray. But how does that look when it actually comes to our prayer time? When using a template like this to pray you recite the first part of the model prayer, and then expand that subject matter with your own thoughts, concerns, and thanksgiving.

An example might look like this:

"'*Hallowed be your name*' - Lord, I beg of you that throughout my day I remember this, and make it my priority as a believer not to reflect you in a negative light. As you know, the meeting I will be attending later will have the possibility of bringing me anger or frustration. Please help me to remember whose son I am, who redeemed me, and who it is I represent... Open my eyes today to how I might make your name holy before others. Separate. Revered."

See how it works? Recite a line out of our template, or model, and then unpack that statement with genuine prayer from your heart while keeping in-line with the direction the model is leading you.

[1] R.C. Sproul offered sound teachings on prayer & many other topics on his daily podcast "Renewing Your Mind" which are still available today at Ligonier Ministries.

Discussion:

1) At the local Christian bookstore, you'll find many, many books on the "correct" way to pray (us talking to God), but relatively few books on how to properly read and understand Scripture (hearing what God is saying to us). What does this say about the priorities and desires of modern day believers?

___

___

___

2) Read Isaiah 52:13 – 53:12. How does this grim reminder of how our Lord saved us affect your view of His name? Does it make you more jealous for His reputation?

___

___

___

___

3) In this chapter, it was stated that the behavior of a professing believer directly affects the purity of the Lord's name before unbelievers. Do you agree with this? Can you think of any examples of a professing believer bringing shame to the name of Christ? Can you think of any examples where you have done this yourself?

___

___

___

___

Discussion (continued):

4) Consider your priorities in prayer. Is it possible to compare them to Scripture and yet avoid turning prayer into a formula and legalistic practice? How are you planning on doing this?

____

____

____

____

____

____

5) Do you align your desires with the written Word and our Lord's priorities when you pray, or do you try to impose your views and priorities on Him?

____

____

____

____

6) In your opinion, who changes their mind the most in prayer, you or the Lord?

____

____

____

____

Chapter 4

His Kingdom

Now that we've come to our heavenly Father and have been reminded to keep the purity of His name as our highest concern, let's continue with our model prayer by looking at the second request:

v10 Your kingdom come, your will be done..."

We will concentrate on the first part of this line before going further, "Your kingdom come". Okay, that sounds nice and all, but what exactly is the kingdom of God? What does this even mean? Well, it can mean a few different things depending on where in Scripture you find the term. The *Westminster Dictionary of Theological Terms* defines it this way:

"God's sovereign reign and rule. God's reign was the major focus of Jesus' teaching. Its' fullness is in the future and yet it has also come in Jesus Himself."[1]

In everyday language, think of it as being God's people in God's place following God's rules and enjoying His blessings.[2]

---

[1] Scriptures cited for this definition are Matt 6:33, Mark 1:15, Luke 6:20, 13:29, 22:18, 10:9 and 17:21

[2] Ligonier Ministries has a great series of articles on the Kingdom, begin here: https://www.ligonier.org/blog/what-kingdom-god/

This means his kingdom isn't limited to just the Heavenly places, but also His people (the church), how they live, and the proclamation of His deeds and glory. Too often people think Heaven is the only Kingdom of God, but this isn't so. Our Lord made it very clear that His kingdom is already everywhere and that He's already seated in it with all authority.[1] Even before His resurrection and ascension, Jesus stated that the kingdom of God had come upon the people of Israel and that this was proven by His miracles.[2] Whether reading Scripture or kneeling in prayer, the Christian must understand that the Kingdom of God isn't just a destination in the after-life. When we come to this in our prayer we are asking that His kingdom be advanced and grown, that His will be carried out here and now.

Practically, this means that we aren't just praying for God to move throughout the world, but also that we ourselves will personally recognize His will and carry it out. This is achieved by reading what He has written and obeying what we find there. This includes the obedience of belief, the striving to live a holy life and our preaching of the Gospel to all people. There can be no doubt that the advancement of God's kingdom includes evangelism for Jesus clearly said He came to save the lost.[3] Because of this (and the great commission[4]) we know that this is a focal point in kingdom work. Of course, the only message that has the "power of God unto salvation" is the true biblical gospel, which includes the message of sin, the justice of God, and the atonement offered by Christ's work on the Cross.[5]

---

[1] Matthew 28:18

[2] Luke 11:20

[3] Luke 19:10

[4] Luke 24:46-47, Acts 1:7-8

[5] Luke 24:47, Mark 16:15 and Romans 1:16

It's the preaching of this message that is one of the primary ways we carry out our Lord's will here on earth. We'll talk about that a little bit more in chapter four.

Another part of bringing in God's Kingdom is when we focus on moving God's will up above of our own. As we do this we experience a shifting in our worldview so that it begins to agree with that of our Lord. An alignment. His will for His kingdom comes ahead of any requests for our own needs. Doing this will no doubt feel quite unnatural and may sometimes bring some serious questions to mind during prayer time. Questions such as:

- Am I kneeling to ask for things on my mind, or that I might seek out the things on His mind?
- Am I more concerned about a relationship I have with a person or how I reflect before others the relationship I have with my savior?
- Am I here just to pray for Uncle Hester's elbow surgery, or also that God gives me the courage and opportunity to share the Gospel with Uncle Hester before the surgery?
- Am I more concerned about my personal health and financial needs, or the needs and spiritual health and needs of local believers, the people in God's kingdom?

We are to seek our Lord's will regarding life's decisions and to ask that He grants repentance and faith to the lost so as to advance His kingdom. We are to be concerned with the mission of His church and the advancement of His will as we live out our lives within the church.

Now that we have some understanding of what the advancement of His kingdom and the accomplishment of His will looks like, let's now look at *how* it's to be done.

"Your kingdom come, your will be done...*on earth as it is in heaven*."

Fallen, sinful men often struggle when it comes time to obey God in all areas of daily life. While it's true that the Christian has been given a new heart at the time of salvation, this new heart is still living in sinful flesh surrounded by a sinful world, and so we struggle.[1] Very often, we struggle a lot! In looking at this line in our prayer we must ask ourselves, "How is God's kingdom expanded and His will carried out in Heaven?" From Scripture we know that His will is carried out joyfully, willingly and with praises given to God for His great wisdom, purity, and glory.[2] The angels do not protest or question His ways! His decrees are carried out without argument, question or compromise. Does this describe how you carry out His will? Does it describe how you as a local community of believers live your lives together and advance His kingdom? Is your evangelism done out of a desire to proclaim the things He has done, or out of guilt? Can you pray this part of the prayer with a sincere heart?

To pray this means you are ready to obey in the same manner as the angels above, to align your desires with the Lord's and to then carry out *His* will with joy. It means you will advance His kingdom with a song in your heart and His praises on His lips. Are you ready for this? Don't be too fast to answer! Take a moment to carefully consider what this means. It means the abandoning of your own goals, rights, and pride.

---

[1] Jeremiah 31:31-34

[2] Deuteronomy 32:1

Talk about an unnatural prayer! Even the personal goals that aren't sinful may not necessarily be in God's will for you at this time. But don't hang on to self and turn back once you've thought this through. Instead, press on! Continue in all sincerity knowing that he who loves his own life will lose it, but he who loses His life for Christ will find it.[1] Embrace His will, and pledge unquestioning obedience. Obey the Lord out of joy, love and a grateful heart knowing that you the believer are in a long line and heritage of those that serve Him.[2] Commit yourself to carrying out His will here on Earth in the same way it is carried out in Heaven.

When we consider the Lord's will and how we should carry it out, we often become aware that we are out of alignment in regards to the priorities of our Lord. In fact, we might sometimes find that we are even in rebellion to His clearly written commands. When praying, whether we become aware that we are guilty of focusing on our personal earthly issues a little too much or if we're suddenly faced with the fact that we don't even consider the priorities of God, the solution is the same. We need to carefully and prayerfully examine His written Word and compare our goals and desires with His. We need to be willing to repent of any priorities we find are out of agreement with those of our Lord, or those that we've put in a higher place than He would have them. This is a humbling exercise, is it not? This kneeling before the throne admitting that we are not the center of our own lives the way we so naturally like to think? Kneeling is a position of humility often used in prayer, but don't be humble in position only! We must also make our proud hearts kneel in humility and submission.

[1] John 12:25

[2] Read Hebrews 11

Remember:

In prayer, consider the mission of the church as a whole and yourself as a member. Then pray that God's will be carried out by all with enthusiasm and joy with the glory of God as the motivation!

Tech Tip!

Remember, this prayer is a model for our daily approach not every prayer that passes through our lips. There is absolutely nothing wrong with dropping to your knees to cry out to God when confronted with a situation (good or bad). We see David model all sorts of different types of prayer in the Psalms. Our daily prayer should bring into alignment our priorities and methods, but it isn't to become a restrictive mandate for every prayer we utter. If you want to cry out to Him in despair, praise, thanksgiving (or whatever else), do it! Just remember to try to discipline yourself to follow the Master's lesson on prayer when you come to your daily scheduled prayer time and then carry the lessons learned there into all prayer. Read the Psalms and note the way the prayers are offered, they are a treasure for those who want to learn to pray!

Discussion:

1) Does the thought of surrendering your will in order to pursue His bring you disappointment and apprehension, or feelings of joy and loyalty? Why do you think you feel the way that you do?

____

____

____

____

Discussion (continued):

2) If, in your prayer time, you find yourself dismissing this model in order to pray your own priorities, what does that say about your worldview? What does it say about Christ's Lordship in your life?

____

____

____

____

____

3) Are the concerns of your heart all earthly? Do you see prayers like yours reflected in the lives and prayers of the New Testament believers? If your prayers are different from Paul, John, Peter and the others, why do you think that is?

____

____

____

____

____

Chapter 5

Supplication

As we move on, we find that we've finally come to the requests for our own practical needs. Needs such as a pretty wife (or handsome husband), new car and plenty of money for junior's college fund are to be offered up at this point in our prayer. Well… maybe not. Let me repeat the key word: *needs*. And not only needs but the things we need to carry out His will (not our own). Let's re-read verse eleven:

Give us this day our daily bread,

Note that this request for needs comes after we have had our priorities realigned. Our model is teaching us to pray for the basics, the things necessary to live as we serve Him. In context of previous lines, this request should be seen as the asking for the supplies necessary to carry out His will. The truth of the matter is that the Christian is a foreigner living in a strange land and should be living with the mindset of a missionary. This isn't our home but rather our mission field. Remember, friend, our home is with our Father and the brothers and sisters that have gone before us. As we obey our Lord's commands and seek to bring about the advancement of His kingdom we will have needs, and it is those needs we are requesting here.

So we need to consider our requests carefully. Some of them may not be sinful in themselves, but if they are for the fulfillment of selfish purposes and not to carry out the Lord's will, then how can such a request be good in God's eyes? For example, a prayer a new automobile isn't a sinful thing. But if our current vehicle is reliable and effective and we simply want a new one because it's shiny and has fun gadgets or features, then the request isn't aimed at our Lord's Kingdom, but on our own pleasures. The "why" of our prayers must be examined as carefully as the "what".

This kind of humble request is drastically different from the methods of prayer taught by modern teachers. There is no hint here that we are to "claim our rights" to bread. Nor are we told that we're to use our authority to "speak" bread into our lives.[1] We aren't even taught that we must have great and bold faith in order to receive bread. Instead, we are simply told to ask our Father to supply us our needs as we carry out His will, trusting that He will provide. When looking into teachings on the subject of prayer, I would encourage you to pay great attention to what Scripture actually teaches. There is often a great gulf between the actual biblical teachings and these new ideas offered by the many teachers now roaming the evangelical landscape.

Simple needs. This is what we're taught to pray for and this should keep us from greed and coveting not only in the prayer closet but also on the street as we go through our day-to-day lives. It also humbles us and takes our eyes off of ourselves.

---

[1] Changing our future through positive words & confessions in an unbiblical tenet of Hinduism that many modern teachers now promote as being Christian.

So we see that once again this prayer might feel unnatural, grating against our sinful nature as its aligning our worldview with that of our Lords. As it guides and teaches us, it continues to keep us focused on His desires and purpose rather than our own. Moving on, we now come to the prayer for forgiveness:

"and forgive us our debts, as we also have forgiven our debtors."

This request for forgiveness is located next to the request for the food we need every day and is even tied to it as part of the same thought. Why? Because we all sin daily (even you, my friend) and we need daily forgiveness for our souls as much as we need physical food for our bodies. I would say even more so! Consider briefly the sins of the last 24 hours. Go ahead…think for a minute. If none spring to mind then quickly review the Ten Commandments[1]. Have you loved and served your God with a 100% devotion every minute of the last day? If not, then you're guilty of breaking the first commandment. Do you have any gods (people or things you love and serve with more attention) in addition to one true God?
If so, then you're guilty of breaking the second commandment. As you can see, we all sin, and sin much. We all need forgiveness, and we need it daily. I would also suggest that it's good to not only meditate on your sins in a general sense and ask our Lord for forgiveness, but also confess the specific sins that come to your mind.[2] In this way we humble ourselves before God and come to rest on His grace alone. It's also good to remember that forgiveness isn't something we receive only when we are first brought to Christ. We receive it at that time and throughout our entire Christian walk as well, with all of it paid for by the blood of Christ.

---

[1] Exodus 20
[2] 1 John 1:9

As much as those who are truly saved hate sin and strive to run from it, we still end up sinning anyway and must come to the Cross begging forgiveness. The forgiveness of sins should always remind us of the gospel, the good news of Christ's work on our behalf.

This is a good place in our prayer to remind ourselves of how we got saved and to consciously turn from sin yet again not to earn salvation, and not even to keep it, but because salvation has already been given. Obedience flows more naturally from gratitude and love than it does from guilt-driven legalism. As we seek forgiveness we should briefly consider how we will separate ourselves from sin as we go forward. Obedience may not bring salvation, but it contributes greatly to our peace.

Notice here we also see the phrase "as we also have forgiven our debtors." Does this mean to be forgiven we must go do something (forgive someone else)? If so, wouldn't that make our forgiveness from God something that we earn? But this can't be true, as we know from clear passages of Scripture that salvation doesn't come from what we do, but from God's grace alone. We looked at Ephesians 2:8-9 earlier in the book, but let's review it again to remind ourselves:

> "For by grace you have been saved through faith. And this is not your own doing; it is the gift of God, not a result of works, so that no one may boast."

As you can see, we are saved through faith by God's grace in the form of a gift (even the faith of a believer is a gift from God).[1] Our good works (such as forgiveness of others) don't contribute at all in a merit-based way so we have no reason to brag.

---

[1] Acts 11:18, 2 Timothy 2:25, Matthew 11:25-27, Ephesians 2:8-9, John 6:65

But before we get confused by this passage and how grace and forgiveness of others fit together, let's take another look at the wording we find here:

"as we also have forgiven our debtors"

The tense used in this line varies between translations. Why? Because there's no easy way to make it accurate in English. The tense used in the Greek manuscripts indicates that forgiving those who offend us isn't just something we have already done before our prayer. It's something that we have already done and are still doing currently, with plans to continue doing as we go forward.[1] This line is highlighting one of the fruits of salvation that has already been made evident in the believer's life, that being the forgiveness of others. Not just for sins of the past, but also the sins that are done against us as we live out our lives, and this makes perfect sense. Like all fruits of the Spirit, forgiveness is something those truly saved do because they are saved, not something they do to become saved.

This phrase about forgiving our debtors, like the phrase immediately before it, is also closely tied to the Gospel. On this part of our prayer, the great commentator Matthew Henry said this, "This is not a plea of merit, but of grace". What he means is that we don't come before the throne pointing to what we have done (forgiven others) and then ask for forgiveness ourselves based on that, but rather we come asking for more grace on top of the grace He's already shown us. Placement of this line here in our daily prayer is to be a reminder that we're not to approach the Father with hate or unforgiveness in our heart.

---

[1] In other words, forgiveness is something we've done and are still doing.

Do not be like the wicked slave who was forgiven of the huge amount he owed, but then went and tortured another man over the small amount that was due him.[1] Our Lord has forgiven you for many, many sins! Will you now approach God while holding grudges? You have done worse to Him, and done it many times over! While forgiveness does indeed come from the heart of the genuine believer, it would be dishonest to say that it's always easy. Christians sometimes struggle with unforgiveness, for often wicked deeds are done towards us. But those who are saved will forgive in the end, for we are being made into our Master's image.[2]

When approaching the throne in prayer, if you are made aware that you have unforgiveness in your heart I would encourage you to lay it down then and there at the feet of God. Reflect on who you were, and the grace God gave you when you were dead in sins and an enemy of God.[3] Give up your rights: your right to be angry, your right to hurt and your right to hate. Give up all such rights to your Master and trust Him to bring mercy and justice where He sees fit. Sometimes this may take years to accomplish, not just a few minutes, but a true follower of Christ will persevere in forgiveness.

We are nearing the end of our model prayer, so let's pay particular attention to how our Lord would have us close:

> 13 And lead us not into temptation, but deliver us from evil.

There are two important things to keep in mind as we read this phrase. The first being that God doesn't tempt us to do evil.[4]

---

[1] Matthew 21:18-35
[2] Ephesians 4:23-24
[3] Ephesians 2:5, Romans 5:10
[4] James 1:13

There is no evil in Him whatsoever, nor does He tempt people to do evil. However, we do see in Scripture that He allows people to be tempted by evil for reasons that sometimes He alone knows (although we know that often it's to build endurance, character and hope in those that follow Him).[1] Some may think this is a small point, but I assure you it isn't! We must always keep in mind our Lord's Holiness, of which purity is a key part. We are to pray God's help in our never-ending job of running away from sin. Notice also that the prayer isn't that He just keeps us from sin but also from temptation. Why? Because when it comes to our own efforts at fighting sin, anyone who has struggled with a particular sin knows it's far easier to avoid situations where temptation might be found than it is to deny that temptation once it's right there in front of them. Run from sin! Not only from sin itself, but even from the places where it may be found!

The second thing we must recognize is that our modern use of the word "tempt" isn't all that's meant here. We think of temptation only as the solicitation to do evil, but the original word held the meaning of "a trial of any kind without reference to its' moral quality."[2] When we come to this line in our prayer, it is best to think of it in its' original and fuller meaning. This is a plea for mercy and the recognition of weakness in regard to the temptation to sin *and* our endurance in hard times.

So here we must pause to consciously recognize that our sovereign Lord who has all knowledge and power is the one who either allows or keeps us from such trials. If we are going through a trial, we must not bury our heads in the sand as so many do and deny that God knew about it or allowed it.

---

[1] 1 Corinthians 10:13, Romans 5:3-4, James 1:2-3

[2] *Vincent's Word Studies in the New Testament*, Hendrickson Publishers

He both knew and allowed, and we must trust His wisdom and purposes above our own and humbly submit that His will be done even if we don't understand it – and even if it hurts. Here we are told to seek Him daily and pray that He keeps us from the temptation to sin so that we might not fall, and from trials so that we might not turn back.

Once again our prayer seems to be acting as our instructor, doesn't it? It's continuing to align us with our Lord's Word and will. In the last few lines, we have been reminded that we sin, that we must seek His forgiveness and that if we are truly reborn we'll have a new heart that is willing and able to forgive others. We have also been reminded to flee from sin, and that we are too weak to do this ourselves and so are in desperate need of divine aid in order to have any success. Lastly, we've been reminded of the sovereignty of God and that all things that happen from either the direct touch of His hand or the granting of His permission.[1]

This next phrase is the last one in our model prayer, and it's somewhat debated:

"For yours is the kingdom and the power and the glory forever. Amen."

Your Bible translation may not even have this line, or it might be there but in brackets or italics. The reason for this is that most of the ancient biblical manuscripts discovered so far don't have it. It's commonly thought that it was an addition put there later, and not part of the original author's writings. Myself, I don't take this matter to be a crucial issue or one that causes me great concern.[2] Why?

---

[1] Job 1:6-12

[2] A good article regarding variations in manuscripts can be found at https://marcminter.com/2017/09/12/is-the-bible-reliable/

Because a simple glance at it tells us it's in complete agreement with the preceding verses, and indeed is a nice summary statement of what I have been calling the "alignment process". It simply tells us that before we close our prayer, we should once again acknowledge that all we are, all we do, and all our goals and dreams should be for the Lord's kingdom instead of our own. It acknowledges that He has all power and should get all the credit and all the glory for the great things He has done. It sends us on our way focused once again on His priorities rather than our own. Another reason that I don't find this issue to be disturbing one is that this line is actually found elsewhere in Scripture. It's a part of an Old Testament prayer and is used in much the same way, as a statement aligning man's desires with those of the Lord.[1] We have one more thing to look at before we're done:

"Amen"

It's a simple word and one that is almost always overlooked, but please don't breeze over it as though it has no meaning. One should always stop and pause before giving an "Amen". That one word of closing means we agree with all that has just been spoken: all the thoughts, confessions, requests and pleas. It means our words are sincere and that we are confident that they line up with God's written Word. So before we stamp our seal of approval here, we must pause for a moment and ask ourselves, "Was everything I just spoke truly genuine and in alignment with my Lord's will?" If it wasn't, repent of those things now before you close out your prayer and go back to daily life! We must be confident that our prayers reflect His will as best we know it.

[1] 1 Chronicles 29:11

Many people also close their prayer with the phrase, "In Jesus' name". This phrase, like the word "Amen", is often spoken out of habit with very little thought as to what it means. Christians are to be acting as the Master's agents or managers here on Earth and when we use this phrase we claim that our prayers have the approval, backing and authority of the one whose name we claim. We should think of ourselves as emissaries or diplomats when we speak. Does every prayer you close using this phrase truly line up with the business and desires of Christ? Here is some food for thought; let's detour from our study in Matthew for a moment to once again look at a passage we read at the start of this book, let's look again at Isaiah 6:1-5

In the year that King Uzziah died I saw the Lord sitting upon a throne, high and lifted up; and the train of his robe filled the temple. [2] Above him stood the seraphim. Each had six wings: with two he covered his face, and with two he covered his feet, and with two he flew. [3] And one called to another and said: "Holy, holy, holy is the LORD of hosts; the whole earth is full of his glory!" [4] And the foundations of the thresholds shook at the voice of him who called, and the house was filled with smoke. [5] And I said: "Woe is me! For I am lost; for I am a man of unclean lips, and I dwell in the midst of a people of unclean lips; for my eyes have seen the King, the LORD of hosts!"

In the New Testament, we learn that the one Isaiah saw sitting on the throne was actually Jesus Christ.[1] Why am bringing up this Old Testament text yet again? I will answer that question with a challenge; when you close a prayer "in Jesus' name" could you do so standing in front of the throne described here? Could you feel the ground shake from His power, see the fearsome creatures proclaiming His Holiness and place your prayer before Him in all confidence that it is in alignment with

[1] John 12:41

His will and purpose? Even imagining ourselves before that throne is a frightening thought! But every time we kneel in prayer that's where we go, even if our outward senses are unaware.[1] So before closing "in Jesus name" take a short pause to think about these things and verify that your words spoken and the deeds you are planning are in agreement with His will.[2]

Please understand, as mortal and sinful people we'll not always know for certain whether or not every request in our prayer is in perfect alignment with our Lord's will. But this shouldn't keep us from praying! Nor should it make us pray nervously or in fear. However, we do need to seek His will out as best we can and strive to pray and live in alignment with it. How to do this is explained in chapter fifteen of the book of John. Verse seven, in particular, explains the confidence we can have in prayer if we are abiding in Christ, that is, truly redeemed and striving to follow His commandments and going about His business instead of our own. Read through that chapter! It's invaluable when trying to understand how to align your will with the Lord's. If we abide in Him, and His Word abides in us (only possible if we regularly study and meditate on it) we can "ask whatever we wish and it will be done" because we will be wishing for the same things as our Master.

If we use our Lord's model prayer and make every effort to conform ourselves to what it teaches we will have taken huge strides in aligning ourselves with Him. Simply put, in life and in prayer He is the Master and we are His subjects that are to be carrying out His business on Earth. Our life and prayers should reflect this.

---

[1] Hebrews 4:16, Revelation 8:4

[2] Colossians 3:17 "And whatever you do, in word or deed, do everything in the name of the Lord Jesus..."

A note on the two verses immediately following:

I think it's important that we take a quick detour to look at the two verses following our model prayer. Why? Because here Jesus gives a lesson on forgiveness, and it is tied to the forgiveness discussed in the model prayer. All the other parts of this prayer are things that should have been familiar to the Jews who were receiving the teaching on that day, but not this part. They had been told that when someone trespasses against them that the law allows and even demands "an eye for an eye".[1] Let's take a quick peek at how Jesus elaborates on this new teaching about forgiveness:

For if you forgive others their trespasses, your heavenly Father will also forgive you, [15] but if you do not forgive others their trespasses, neither will your Father forgive your trespasses. *Matthew 6:14-15*

What should we make of this? Again, the first reading would seem to indicate that if we ourselves want forgiveness we must go and perform good deeds, that we must forgive others in order to be forgiven. We already looked at this topic a little bit and saw that forgiveness is something that flows from a genuine salvation and believers live it out for the rest of their lives. To understand this in greater detail let's remind ourselves what happens when we are saved. After that, we'll look into a teaching about how we live our lives as Christians today.

So, let's first remind ourselves of the Gospel message and the effects of true conversion. The Gospel message is "repentance and the forgiveness of sins" in Jesus name.[2] It's the good news message that comes after the bad news.

---

[1] Exodus 21:23-24

[2] Luke 24:47

The bad news is that we are all guilty of crimes against God's law and the penalty for those crimes must be paid. The judge is just, and cannot simply pardon the guilty because justice won't allow it.[1] The good news (gospel) is that we have a rescuer, Jesus Christ, who paid that penalty for His people when He hung on the Cross. When we recognize and turn from all sin trusting that He and He alone will pay the penalties due, His payment is put on our account and we are given right-standing before the Heavenly Court.[2] In other words, our rescuer switches places with us and pays the fines due Himself. This transaction happens when we repent and believe (trust). When saved the believer is re-made, or born again[3] into a completely new person with a new heart and the Spirit of God living inside them.[4] Salvation is a new legal standing before the High Court, but it's also a complete transformation of the one saved. After this transformation, the believer obeys God out of a desire to do so which means we not only repent when coming to Christ, but we also live a life of repentance because we want to obey God and flee from sin.

Now, what does this all have to do with forgiveness? A lot! Why? Because in other passages we see Jesus directly commands us to forgive others.[5] What this means is that to hold onto unforgiveness is not only unhealthy, but it's a sin. A true Christian will want to forgive (although sometimes it's difficult) because they've already been re-made and are still being changed.[6]

---

[1] Proverbs 17:15

[2] He confirmed the success of this mission, His deity, and His sinlessness when He rose again from the dead.

[3] John 3:1-8

[4] Ezekiel 36:25-28, Jeremiah 31:33-34

[5] Luke 17:3-4, Matthew 18:21-22

[6] Philippians 2:13

They want to forgive not only because they have been told to, but because they want to as they are keenly aware of how many sins they themselves have been forgiven.[1] A true Christian will live a life of repentance which means walking away from sin and this includes the sin of unforgiveness. Or in other words, holding onto unforgiveness in one's heart would indicate a lack of repentance. Someone embracing it could hardly be said to have recognized and turned from this sin when they are still stubbornly holding it, right? Here, Jesus isn't teaching us "go do this stuff and then I'll save you". Instead, He's simply highlighting that unforgiveness as a sin which needs to be turned from the same as all other sins when we repent and believe.

We can hardly come to the throne to ask forgiveness for sin when we are intentionally and stubbornly persisting in sin even as we kneel. Let's use another sin as a way to illustrate this point. If someone told you they've come to trust Christ as their savior and have repented of all sin, but they refuse to give up their habit of murdering people, would you believe they had repented of sin? Of course not! When a person intentionally continues to hang on to sin it shows they have not received the gift of repentance and have not been saved.[2] If you're struggling with unforgiveness you need to recognize it as a sin and turn from it today. Letting go of unforgiveness is often a struggle, but it's a struggle that your Lord is calling you to make.

Another way to look at this passage is to think of how we are taught to live out our lives as Christians. Consider the teaching we are given later in Matthew, the account of Jesus washing the feet of the disciples in chapter 13.

---

[1] Matthew 18:23-35

[2] Repentance, like faith, is a gift - 2 Timothy 2:25, Acts 11:18, Galatians 2:8-9

Jesus tells Peter that the disciples were "clean", indicating that they were truly saved (although the Master was careful to point out that one of them wasn't). He then insisted that while they were clean as a person, their feet were not clean (they had been traveling as they followed Him to the feast). When this passage is fully studied, we learn Jesus was using foot washing as an analogy of the Christian life. It taught that while the Spirit had indeed saved them and cleansed them from sin, in the Christian life dirt (sin) is often picked up again as we go and it must be cleaned once more.

To be clear, this isn't teaching multiple salvation events. Once a person is saved their salvation isn't lost every time they sin but instead it shows that we must be continually cleansed by the Spirit which is often symbolized in Scripture by water. Applying this teaching here we learn that we must be willing to turn from unforgiveness (and all sin) when we come to our Lord in prayer and humble ourselves to His Spirit as He leads us in repentance and grace.

Well, our short detour into the subject of unforgiveness turned into a long detour and so now we need to turn it around so we can wrap up this chapter.

Remember:
We forgive others because we have been forgiven much, because He told us to, and because we are to live a life of repentance as we follow Christ knowing all sin harms our relationship with God and the effectiveness of our prayers.[1]

[1] Psalm 66:18

Tech Tip!

It's not about you. That could be a summary sentence describing the alignment process we saw in the Disciple's Prayer, and it should be a guideline as we follow our Lord's model. Our desires, goals, praise, and requests should all be focused on our Lord and His kingdom, not our own. He made us and then we rebelled. But rather than destruction, He sent a rescue that cost Him His own blood. Even our forgiveness of others is because of Him and for Him. Keep these incredible truths in mind as you pray. It's not about you.

Discussion:

1) When praying for your needs, do you think in terms of what you need to do His will His way, or do you think of your needs in terms of what you need to accomplish your own goals and dreams?

____

____

____

____

2) What influences your prayers more, the Bible or earthly life? Can you think of some steps you can take to bring your prayers more in alignment with our Lord and His Word?

____

____

____

____

Discussion (continued):

3) Is avoiding temptation to sin something that you consciously think about and seek the Lord's help? If avoiding sin doesn't seem to be on your priorities when you pray, why do you think that is?

____

____

____

____

4) List a few goals and dreams for your life below. Now ask yourself if they are they are focused on building His kingdom or your own. Answer honestly!

____

____

____

____

5) Do you have a person that you are struggling to forgive? Have you gone to the Lord in prayer asking His help in repenting of this sin and helping you to go forward in forgiveness?

____

____

____

____

Discussion (continued):

6) If you have never asked the Lord's help to forgive somebody, why is that? Will you commit now to moving forward on this?

____

____

____

____

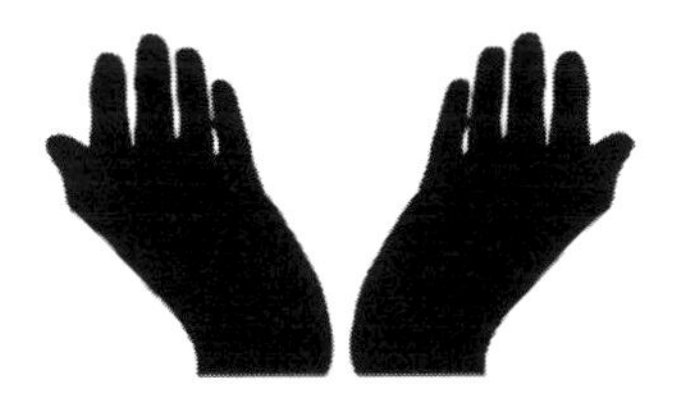

Chapter 6

Thanksgiving And Praise

I'm not sure if you noticed, but there isn't anything in our model prayer regarding the role of thanksgiving and praise. That being said, it's hard not to notice that just about everywhere else in Scripture we see people praising our Lord and giving Him thanks. It happens a lot. A whole lot! Before we run off to see what can be learned about this, we need to take note that thanksgiving and praise are two different things. Most folk in our day haven't put a ton of thought into these two terms, but they can be understood this way:

Thanksgiving – This is giving thanks or vocalizing gratitude for the things that our Lord has promised, said and/or done.

Praise – This would be vocalizing admiration and/or wonderment at who our Lord is, what He is like and the things He has done. It's a written or vocal appreciation of His attributes.

Diving into this subject won't take a lot of time, but it will take us on a brief tour of some passages in Scripture. But before we look at what we see there, please let me throw my two cents about thanksgiving on the table right at the start:

How Can We *Not* Be Thankful?!?

I don't know about you, but I sin. A LOT! I have committed many, many sins in my past and it breaks my heart to say it, but I'm sure I will be sinning some more again tomorrow. No matter how hard I try, I still mess up. I don't mess up quite as bad as I used to (thanks to the patient work of our Lord) but I still sin a bunch. To say otherwise would be not only prideful, it would also be a lie. And then I would have some more pride and lies tacked on to the already impressive list of sins I've racked up over the years! So what does my sin, and your sin, have to do with thanksgiving in prayer? I'm glad you asked!

For all who truly belong to Christ (those who have been bought by His blood), gratitude and thanksgiving should be natural and passionate. Think of the sins we have committed, yet our Lord still saved us! He knew every nasty thing we would ever say, think or do and yet saved us anyway. He even knew of the sins you will commit three Tuesdays from now, sins that haven't even crossed your mind yet! And He still went to that Cross. How can we *not* be thankful? This is an amazing thing! How can we not overflow with gratitude? And if that is our state of mind, how can this not come out when we take time to talk to Him in prayer?

Truly, it's easy to see why the Apostle Paul seemed to look at thanksgiving and gratitude as signs of a true believer.[1] If you have no such thoughts or emotions, I would recommend you take some time now to think of your sins, to think of the sacrifice made on your behalf, and to examine where you stand.

---

[1] Romans 1:21

Now, let's dig in! I won't spend a lot of time pointing out every single instance in Scripture that a follower can be seen giving thanks when talking to God. Instead, I will simply ask you to take a moment to think for yourself how often you have seen it when reading. Just think of the crazy life of King David if you need a place to start. More than once he found himself the object of disrespect and hatred, even to the point where he was hunted like a dog. Yet when He cried out to our Lord, he would also give thanks and show an incredible and emotional gratitude in both the words and spirit of his prayers. Consider David's words in just a few of the Psalms he wrote:[1]

But I will sing of your strength; I will sing aloud of your steadfast love in the morning. For you have been to me a fortress and a refuge in the day of my distress. O my Strength, I will sing praises to you, for you, O God, are my fortress, the God who shows me steadfast love.

That was written while David was being hunted by men with orders to kill him! This next one was written while David was a prisoner of Israel's arch-enemy the Philistines:[2]

This I know, that God is for me. In God, whose word I praise, in the Lord, whose word I praise, in God I trust; I shall not be afraid. What can man do to me? I must perform my vows to you, O God; I will render thank offerings to you. For you have delivered my soul from death, yes, my feet from falling, that I may walk before God in the light of life.

---

[1] Psalm 59:16-17

[2] Psalm 56:9-13

And this next Psalm was written while hiding in a cave while troops searched for him to kill him:[1]

> I will give thanks to you, O Lord, among the peoples; I will sing praises to you among the nations. For your steadfast love is great to the heavens, your faithfulness to the clouds. Be exalted, O God, above the heavens! Let your glory be over all the earth!

If the writings of David don't persuade you of how naturally both thanksgiving and praise flows from a true follower (regardless of circumstances), then think of how often we see the writers of the New Testament letters giving thanks to God when they wrote letters to fellow believers. If they are thanking the Lord constantly when writing to each other, I think we can safely assume that they thank God even more when speaking directly to Him! Often, these men were writing from prison or on the run. They were despised and hunted because of their faith and yet praise and gratitude seem to pour out of them. Even when the Apostle Paul was in prison waiting for his death sentence to be carried out, he began a letter like this:[2]

> I thank God whom I serve, as did my ancestors, with a clear conscience, as I remember you constantly in my prayers night and day.

As you can see, while there isn't a clear command in the Lord's Prayer telling us to praise our God and give Him thanks, but we can hardly look at the pages of Scripture without seeing it modeled before us.[3] Logically speaking, the forgiveness of our sins should drive every one of us to thanksgiving.

---

[1] Psalm 57:9-11

[2] 2 Timothy 1:3

[3] Psalm 150 may be taken as a clear command to praise our Lord, or it may be viewed as a rallying cry or encouragement. Either way, let us praise Him!

Biblically, we see that praise and thanksgiving seem to flow from practically every believer. Personally, all we have to do is reflect on the greatness, majesty, and mercy of the Lord of Hosts and we will naturally be inclined to give passionate and genuine praise and thanks to our Lord who is so worthy and has done so much!

In short, we should be giving thanks when we pray. Even in the worst of times, when death might be mere moments away, we cannot help but recognize that we are incredibly blessed and the recipients of so much more than we deserve! We also need to open ourselves up to marveling at who He is and giving Him the praise He is due for what He is like and the things He has done. When we pray, let it be with praise and thanksgiving!

<u>Discussion:</u>

1) In Romans 1:21 Paul seems to imply that not giving thanks to God for even the most simple of life's provisions is a sign of a person being an unbeliever. How does this affect your view of gratitude in prayer?

 ____

 ____

 ____

2) Do your prayers usually include a good deal of gratitude and thanks or are they mostly requests? What adjustments might be necessary?

 ____

 ____

 ____

Chapter 7

Knowing the Will of God

Earlier, as we were finishing our look at the Lord's Prayer, I briefly mentioned that we can't always know for certain the will of God in every circumstance. While a deep knowledge and love of Scripture will guide us in most situations, there are always choices to be made in areas that aren't specifically discussed in our Bibles. So what are we to do when faced with such choices? We know that we are to do what our Master wants us to do, but how do we do that when there is no clear direction given to us? Rather than try to answer that question myself, I thought it best to turn to one who has for years been recognized as an outstanding authority on the subject of prayer. I'm talking about a man that not only lived his own life in complete dependence on God for each and every meal but also ran orphanages that housed thousands of children with often no money whatsoever on hand. Every day he would simply pray, trusting that the needs of his family and the children he looked after would be met. That man is George Mueller and we'll now look at what he wrote on knowing God's will. He shares seven simple steps, and they're invaluable:[1]

[1] Steps are an excerpt from George Mueller's "Answers to Prayer" by Moody Classics, 2007. I would highly recommend this book. Good stuff!

1. I seek at the beginning to get my heart into such a state that it has no will of its' own in regard to a given matter. Nine-tenths of the trouble with people generally is right here. Nine-tenths of the difficulties are overcome when our hearts are ready to do the Lord's will, whatever it may be. When one is truly in this state, it's usually but a little way to the knowledge of what His will is.

2. Having done this, I do not leave the result to feeling or simple impressions. If so, I make myself open to great delusions.

3. I seek the will of God through, or in connection with, the Word of God. The Spirit and the Word must be combined. If I look to the Spirit alone without the Word, I make myself open to great delusions also. If the Holy Spirit guides us at all, He will do it according to Scriptures and never contrary to them.

4. Next, I take into account providential circumstances. These often plainly indicate God's will in connection with His Word and His Spirit.

5. I ask God in prayer to reveal His will to me plainly.

6. And so through prayer to God, the study of the Word and reflection, I come to a deliberate judgment according to the best of my ability and knowledge. If my mind is then at peace and continues in peace after two or three more petitions, I proceed accordingly. In both trivial matters, and in those that are most important issues, I have found this method always effective.

Discussion:

1) George Mueller states that he gets his heart into a state where it has "no will of its' own." Are you able to do this, or do you see your personal desires as being too strong? If you can't do this, what does that say about your priorities?

____

____

____

____

____

2) Do you have such knowledge of the written Word that you usually know the path you are to take, or do you regularly struggle with decisions only to find out later that the Word covers such issues?

____

____

____

____

____

Discussion (continued):

3) Does providencc[1] truly help us know the will of God? What do you see in Scripture as far as providence and His will?[2]

____

____

____

____

____

4) Do you see yourself being able to take these steps in seeking God's will, or do you think it likely that emotion and personal desire will be more influential than they should? What steps can you take to be more in alignment with Mueller's method?

____

____

____

____

____

[1] Providence – The idea that God governs all things and will make the ways & supplies available for one to follow the path He intends for one to follow.

[2] Proverbs 3:6, Psalm 103:19, Matthew 10:29, Luke 1:52, Acts 17:26, Psalm 4:8

Chapter 8

Prayer – Putting it All together

Before we finish this little study on prayer, let's take a moment to look at the big picture of how real prayer flows both from, and to, our Lord. Scripture tells us that when a person is redeemed, the Spirit of God begins living inside them and leads them in their thoughts and actions.[1] Their heart of stone is made to live, to feel, and this brings about a life trademarked by increasing loyalty and obedience to their Lord.[2] As you can see, genuine salvation brings about a lot of change! One part of the change is that to some degree (often small at first but ever increasing) a desire for prayer now flows naturally from the Christian. Not only prayer, but prayer in agreement with the will of the Master. A new believer may only pray for themselves at first and might even offer prayers for some pretty odd things, but it isn't long before their prayers began to be for others and to also be more in-line with the will of God. Why? Because the Holy Spirit inside them is changing, leading and maturing them. Prayers that felt unnatural at first become comfortable.

The Spirit wants genuine prayer to be offered, prayers that will be heard and honored. Did I just say heard? Indeed I did! Take a look at this passage:

---

[1] Ezekiel 36:26-27, Romans 8:14

[2] 2 Corinthians 5:17, John 14:21-24, Jeremiah 31:33, Ephesians 4:30

This is the confidence that we have toward him, that if we ask anything according to his will he hears us. And if we know that he hears us in whatever we ask, we know that we have the requests that we have asked of him. *1 John 5:14-15*

Did you see that? It is when we ask according to His will that He hears us. Of course, this passage is using the word "hear" to mean "hear and be attentive", not just the physical act of hearing alone. The creator of the universe doesn't need a hearing aid! This verse sounds odd to some people when they first read it. It's against the beliefs and teachings of many to suggest that God doesn't listen carefully and give consideration to all prayers, but that is clearly what this passage tells us. And it makes perfect sense if we think about it. Our sovereign God, who has all knowledge and power, would never consider sinful or self-serving prayers that are out of alignment with His own values and desires. So are all of your prayers in perfect alignment with Him? No? Me neither! The truth of the matter is that none of us are sinless or perfected yet and so all of us, even mature believers, often fall short by praying for that which doesn't align with God's will. Or sometimes we fail to pray at all! Our transformation and alignment with God did indeed start when He converted us, but it will continue on throughout our lives.

This is why every time we come to our Father in prayer we must examine our motives, desires and our goals. We must also discipline ourselves to have time set aside every day when we can use His model and approach His throne. When we kneel in prayer we must remind ourselves that our salvation was by Him and for Him, and so our prayers should reflect that our lives are kingdom focused not self-focused.

Believers have been saved by God the Son and are now filled with God the Holy Spirit. They are being changed to become increasingly holy and pure, and their prayers to God the Father will reflect all of this. It is during this process of change that praying the way our Lord teaches can sometimes feel unnatural. But we must continue to align ourselves with His teaching, remembering that the hand of our triune God is on every aspect of true prayer which is why we would be crazy not to seek out more prayer time! There are very few things in this world that can draw us closer to our Lord than genuine prayer! It's all about Him. We're to perform all worship, including prayer, in spirit and in truth which means we need to allow ourselves to be guided by both the Holy Spirit and the written Word.[1]

If we find ourselves reluctant to pray, it's good to examine those feeling. If we don't want to approach God's throne due to fear or shame because of sin, then the need for prayer is even greater! Shove aside the reluctance and find a private place to cry out for to Him. We can't allow our sin to keep us from approaching the God who forgives. This is also a good time to remind ourselves that it isn't our moral performance that saves us or keeps us saved. Whether we fall into a sin or not, it was the sacrifice of the sinless Son of God that saves His people, not how well we did that day.

Closing it Out

Now that you know a little bit more about prayer and have a great model to follow, let me ask you this; can you approach the holy and awesome throne and pray our Lord's priorities in a godly way and do it sincerely? Will you allow yourself to be "realigned" so that your views begin to agree with the views of God?

---

[1] John 4:24, John 17:17

When you close your prayer with "In Jesus Name" will that statement be accurate? Remember also that prayer is only half of our conversation with God. While we must take great care in speaking to Him, we must also be diligent to hear from Him as well by reading the message He has sent us. So many people in these modern times are desperately trying to receive direct revelations and have mystic conversations with God, but seldom take the time to do that which is easy and trustworthy ; pick up the Bible and read it! If you truly want a "God encounter" this is the way to have one without any worry of being led astray by others, or even by yourself.

I hope this book has helped teach you to pray but I also hope it has shown you how *not* to pray. Prayers performed out of religious habit with the expectation of somehow earning something are useless and so also are prayers given while stubbornly holding onto sin or those focused on our own desires rather than His.[1] It's tricky to teach and encourage prayer without falling into legalism but I hope this was accomplished. Isaiah told us that our Lord is near to those who are of sincere, humble and contrite heart.[2] Don't make your Father puzzle in wonder and amazement at your lack of prayer any longer. He wants to hear from you!

Remember:

It isn't complicated! Prayer is to be sincere, from the heart, and in alignment with the teachings and will of our Lord as clearly taught in Scripture. If these things are remembered, you'll be on the right track!

[1] Matthew 6:5-7, Psalms 66:18
[2] Isaiah 66:2

Discussion:

1) Did looking at the Scriptures presented in this book change how you pray? If so, how?

____

____

____

____

____

2) Are you going to begin to pray daily?

____

____

____

____

3) If you had to write yourself a note, a reminder, of what to keep in mind every day before you kneel down to seek the Lord, what would that note say?

____

____

____

____

____

PRAYER

As you head down the road…

If we were to sum up this whole book in one sentence it would be this: *It's all about Him!* If we are truly following Jesus Christ it's because He has changed us from the sinful, self-loving people we used to be into folks who love and follow Him, the One who saved us. We are no longer the focus of our own lives, He is now our focus– and this will be reflected not only in the choices we make but also in how we pray (as well as how we live life, read scripture, and even relax). We will want to pray "unnatural" prayers that focus on His will over our own.

If you're looking for some reading that addresses various aspects of prayer and some of the errors that are all-too-common, check out these titles:

A Simple Way to Pray	by Martin Luther
Call Unto Him	by Charles H. Spurgeon
Prayer	by John Bunyan
Truth or Territory?	by Jim Osman
A Time of Departing	by Ray Yungen

APPENDIX A

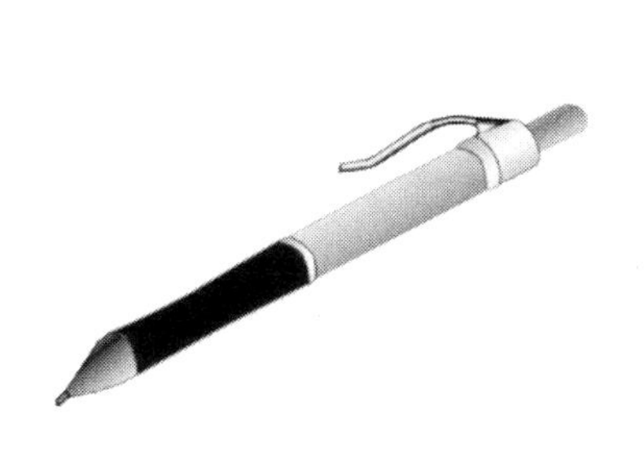

Various articles that might be of interest

WHAT IS A TRUE CHRIST-FOLLOWER? ARE YOU ONE? AM I? WHAT THE BIBLE SAYS ABOUT WHAT MAKES A TRUE FOLLOWER

You may be reading this little article, but I'm betting there's a good chance that some of you aren't real excited about reading it. Is this you? Are you fighting the temptation to skip it and go somewhere "more interesting"? I understand if that's how you feel. If you already consider yourself to be a follower of Jesus you may think that reading about who followers are will be dull at best. You might just be reading the first few lines so as to say you looked at it with the idea of flipping forward in a few minutes. Before you move on because you think this bit isn't necessary (for you), let me remind you that the Apostle Paul himself told folks they needed to examine and test themselves to see if they were really in the faith.[1] It's interesting to note that he made that statement in a letter *after* he identified them as people he thought were genuine believers.

Have you had the Apostle Paul personally write you a letter stating that he considers you to be a solid believer? No? Me neither! Even if he had, that would only mean that I too need follow his direction and examine myself to see if I'm *truly* in the faith. In other words – don't skip this material.

---

[1] 2 Corinthians 13:5

We all need to take a pause and test ourselves to find where our beliefs and affections are truly found. So let's look at this idea of being a follower…

What is a follower? Is it the same thing as being a Christian? Do we even want to be called "Christian" when there are so many folks out there claiming to be Christian that are doing and saying things that appear to be very *unlike* what Jesus said and did? If that's the case then I don't know what to call anyone, including myself. Why? Because if we're honest, you and I don't always live up to His example either! So are they hypocrites or true followers of Christ? What am I? I don't know about you, but I'm getting confused! What we call someone who believes the teachings of Jesus Christ probably has more to do with some modern social understanding of words rather than real definitions. I've even heard people say there is a difference between someone who follows Christ and a Christ follower. But maybe all this stems from a faulty viewpoint. Maybe we are looking at this wrong and don't truly understand what makes a person a Christian, or a true follower. With so many people claiming to be followers, disciples, Christians, pilgrims, etc. and doing some very different things, it makes you wonder.

After all, anyone can claim to be a Christian. Hitler, Mussolini and Stalin all claimed to be Christians at different points in their lives as well as the many men who launched and fought in the blood-thirsty crusades. But for this little book I'm going to ask that you put all that aside. Here, we will use the words "follower" and "Christian" interchangeably. Why? To avoid confusion! Biblically speaking, if someone is *truly* following after Christ and His teachings, then they are defined as "Christian".

As far as I'm concerned, if that word is good enough for the Apostles and first generation believers, it's good enough for me!

Now that we cleared that up – are you one? Am I? There's only one way to find out what we truly are and that's to look at the definition of what a Christian is according to the only reliable source. What source? Well, the Bible of course! (Please tell me you got that one right?!?) So what is taught in Scriptures? What does a follower look like? What is a Christian? The first use of the word "Christian" is found in Acts 11:26 where the followers of Christ and His teaching were given that name by the residents of Antioch after their beliefs and actions had become well-known. The word meant "little Christs" and can be viewed as a slang word for people who walked (lived) the way he walked. They imitated Him as they followed after Him. So a true Christian or follower is one who follows the teachings of Christ and lives in a way that is like Christ. Of course, Jesus taught a lot of things during the three years He was a public figure, right?

So the next logical question is "What teachings did the people of Antioch hear to cause them to call His followers 'little Christs'"? Well, they probably heard a lot of Christ's material but we can be confident that the primary message was the Gospel.[1] The Gospel is the message Jesus specifically told His followers to spread in the book of Luke.[2] Conveniently enough, the content of Jesus' message was later clearly defined by the Apostle Paul when he wrote his first letter to the Corinthians.[3]

---

[1] The word "Gospel" means "good news"

[2] Luke 24:47

[3] 1 Corinthians 15:1-11, check it out – it's a great passage to know!

The Gospel is the message that God uses to bring a person to Himself. It's the message that must be truly believed and treasured and is the only message described in Scripture as being the "power of God unto salvation".[1] The Gospel message is indeed a message of "good news". What makes it so good, you ask? That's easy! It isn't a message of what we must go do, but rather a message of what has been done for us. You may think it sounds odd that becoming a Christian isn't something we are supposed to go do since it's often preached that way. But it shouldn't sound odd at all! Why? Because there's absolutely nothing that we *can* do to make ourselves right with God! We're all guilty before God and we have no way whatsoever to earn His approval. We cannot "straighten up and fly right". It's too late for that! We are already guilty of sins![2] This may sound harsh or alarming as in recent years there have been a lot of teachers coming forward to tell us that we aren't all *that* guilty before God and people are basically good at heart. The theme of modern preaching seems to be that God's biggest problem is getting us to love, behave and live up to our highest potential. While this sounds nicer than some of the fire and brimstone sermons of the past, if we want to be true Christ followers we need to turn to Scripture to see what *it* teaches.

So let's take a look and see if we are true followers, true Christians, by seeing if we believe the most basic and primary teaching Jesus gave – the Gospel. According to the third chapter of the New Testament book Romans every single one of us is guilty of sin.[3]

---

[1] Romans 1:16

[2] **ATTENTION**: Footnotes provide a *LOT* of info in this book. Be sure to check em' out!

[3] Romans 3:10-18.While Paul moved the pen in the writing of Romans, the Holy Spirit is the true author. This same Holy Spirit is part of the Trinity along with the Father & Son. When the Trinity is understood, it's clear Jesus had a hand in writing ALL Scripture!

Now, we use the word "sin" when discussing these things but exactly what is sin?[1] An easy-to-use definition of sin is any thought or activity that breaks the law of God.[2]
A good summary of God's law can be found in the Ten Commandments.[3] Even a quick review of them will make us aware that we're all guilty. Really guilty!

Every one of us has told at least one lie, pursued our own will instead of God's, lusted, stolen, spoken evil words, and a whole lot more. So, when we say "sin" we are really referring to things that are seen as crimes in God's court, crimes against His law. If a just judge here on earth judged us according to God's laws, he would have to pronounce us guilty or he wouldn't be just. The judge may love the guilty man, may feel sympathy for the man, may recognize that the man has stopped committing as many crimes as he once did, but none of these things have any effect on the punishment that must be handed down for crimes already committed. If a crime has been committed, the fine must be paid. Period. Time, love and regret do not pay for past crimes. And isn't God more just than any earthly judge?[4] He is! God must punish those who have broken His righteous law (sinned) and Hell is the place that is not only fitting but also the place designated by the lawmaker. It's a place of eternal torment, pain and regret. A place filled not with the fleshly pleasures of sin, but of their consequences. It is filled with hate, pain, darkness and fear and will remain that way for all eternity. Contrary to many modern-day teachings, the reality of Hell is taught throughout Scripture.

---

[1] A fuller definition of sin can be found in the Westminster Catechism, "Sin is any want of conformity unto, or transgression of, the law of God." See also 1 John 3:4

[2] Paul refers to the Ten Commandments as the "law" in Romans 7:7b

[3] The Ten Commandments are listed Exodus 20.

[4] Proverbs 17:15 teaches us clearly that God will never pardon the guilty.

If you look down to the footnotes on the bottom of this page you'll find several references to where Hell is taught as being the real and final destination for those who continue in their rebellion against the holy and just God, but it's far too big a topic to cover here.[1] The point is this: When a guilty man is standing before a just judge who knows the law, that judge must hand down the punishment due, or he will no longer be just.

I know you may be asking yourself, "What does this have to do with the gospel and following Christ?" Well…lots! You'll see in just a second. And I also understand the confusion behind that question; so far I've been telling you *bad* news and the gospel is supposed to be *good* news. Sorry about that! It's never pleasant to hear that you (like all humans) are in big, big trouble and there's nothing you can do to fix it. The judge is just, He is all-knowing, all-powerful and we are all guilty. But that bad news *had* to be delivered before the good news of the gospel made any sense. So what exactly does the Bible say the good news is?

What is the message that changes us from guilty lawbreakers with no hope into a God-fearing Christian man or woman who wants to follow Christ? What's this message that all true followers believe and treasure? It is this:

Wait, wait, wait! I'm sorry, but before we look at that I have to ask – *are you still with me*? Can you say that to this point you are agreeing with Scripture when it says that you, I and everyone else is guilty??[2] Do you also understand that Hell is the real and designated "resting" place for those who turn in disbelief and/or rebellion?

---

[1] Matthew 25:41-46, Jude 7, Matthew 3:12, Also see website Carm.Org/Hell

[2] If not, review Romans 3:9-18 or the 10 Commandments in Exodus 20. ALL are guilty!

If not, go back through the last page or two and look up the footnote Scripture references and see for yourself. In context, it's pretty clear. I'm not making this stuff up!! So if you're still on board, let's look at the Gospel message. Here it is:

The death of Jesus Christ on the Cross.

That is the good news for His people! It may be hard to think that the torture and murder of an innocent man could be called "good news", but once you understand what it was all about you, might call it good too. You'll probably even call it great! You see, crimes have been committed and for the judge to remain just, the penalties for those crimes must be paid. No man or woman has any hopes of paying those penalties on their own, just as cleaning up now doesn't pay for crimes in the past. As mentioned before, it's too late for all that! For anyone to be saved, the penalty for their crimes (sins) must be paid by someone else. They must be rescued. That is what the good news gospel message is; it's the news of a rescue that has been worked out by our Lord to save His people from their sin and its' consequence.

So what did this rescue do, how did it work? I'm glad you asked! I can answer that question with one word – Atonement.[1] When Christ suffered and died, He paid the fine for His people. He took the fine, the punishment, on Himself so that those who were guilty were made to be in right-standing with the High Court. The fine that you and I could never pay has been paid by someone else! Now do you see why the Cross is good news? It's a rescue for the helpless! This atonement could never be earned and it is only offered as a gift that must be received by faith.

---

[1] CARM.org online dictionary defines atonement as removal of man's guilt. For more on atonement see Romans 5:6-11

The payment of fines is applied to your account when you give up all hope of trying to pay it yourself through good behavior, cleaning up, religious acts, or whatever else and trust Jesus Christ alone to pay your debt. Completely and totally trust in His work over your own, it is only then that the payment is applied.[1] That's the good news of the gospel – that salvation is available for those who repent and believe. Uh-oh! Did I just lose you? I added something to belief, didn't I? I added the word "repent". Why would I do that? Well, because Jesus told us we are supposed to preach repentance as a mandatory part of forgiveness.[2]

Now, before you start thinking that because I've added the word "repent" that I'm saying good works are a necessary requirement for salvation, let me clarify what the word "repent" means. It means to change your mind in regard to sin. To recognize sin (all sin, not just the really bad ones) as wicked and make the decision to turn from them. To repent isn't to *do* anything; it's a decision about what you will do and not do in the future. Many think to repent is to feel sorrow for your sins, but that's inaccurate as well. A true change of mind will indeed bring sorrow for past sin, but a lot of people feel really bad about their sins and still don't turn from them.
If you're interested, there's a more detailed article about the meaning of repentance at the back of this book.[3]

So that's the good news - for one who trusts in Christ's work on the Cross, turns from sin and stops trying to rescue themselves, they will end up being rescued by one who paid a great price do to so.

---

[1] Romans chapter 4
[2] Luke 24:47
[3] *"What Does the Word Repent Mean"* located in Appendix A

Actually, that's only *part* of the good news. That's the part traditionally called "the gospel" but there's much more good news than that, and it has a lot to do with how we can tell if we are true Christ-followers. When a person is truly forgiven (saved, born-again, adopted, made into a disciple /follower) that person doesn't just receive a "change of status" stamp on some piece of heavenly paperwork. The person is changed. When the Old Testament prophets Ezekiel and Jeremiah were describing it, they said it like this:

"Then I will sprinkle clean water on you, and you will be clean. Your filth will be washed away, and you will no longer worship idols.[26] And I will give you a new heart, and I will put a new spirit in you. I will take out your stony, stubborn heart and give you a tender, responsive heart. [27] And I will put my Spirit in you so that you will follow my decrees and be careful to obey my regulations" *Ezekiel 36:25-27*

"I will put my instructions deep within them, and I will write them on their hearts. I will be their God, and they will be my people.[34] And they will not need to teach their neighbors, nor will they need to teach their relatives, saying, 'You should know the LORD.' For everyone, from the least to the greatest, will know me already," says the LORD. "And I will forgive their wickedness, and I will never again remember their sins." *Jeremiah 31:33-34*

Do you see what happens to a person when they become a true Christian? They are changed at a foundational level! The heart hardened by sin is removed and a new heart is given. They start obeying God's laws out of a love for God and His ways rather than an effort to earn something. <u>This means obedience is what flows from salvation, not something that takes you to it.</u>

The Spirit of God begins to live in that person and guide them. In the New Testament in the book of 1st John we are told what this looks like in a person's day-to-day life, and how we can know if we are true disciples (truly saved):

And we can be sure that we know him if we obey his commandments.[4] If someone claims, "I know God," but doesn't obey God's commandments, that person is a liar and is not living in the truth.[5] But those who obey God's word truly show how completely they love him. That is how we know we are living in him.[6] Those who say they live in God should live their lives as Jesus did." *1 John 2:3-6*

Do you see what it says? It says that a true follower will have a life trademarked by obedience to God, not sin. That a true Christ-follower will walk the way Christ walked. And how did He walk? He had a love for His Brothers and Sisters (Christians), met with them regularly, obeyed God, and had a love of the written Word while having no love for the things or opinions of the world. If you read the whole book of 1st John you will see that a lot of these things are actually given as signs so you will know if you truly know Him or have deceived yourself.

And so now, dear reader, I must ask you to examine yourself in the same way I must examine myself. Do these things describe you? I know you are not perfect and sinless, and neither am I; that's covered in 1st John, too. But what does your overall life look like? Do you ignore known sins and shun those who are Christians while seldom reading the written Word? Be honest! What about obedience and your motives for it? A person's motives say a lot!

As you can see, the Bible gives us a very clear picture of what a true follower believes, and does, and the changes that have been made to them. To say that a person can be a follower of Jesus and not believe the gospel is ridiculous. It's like saying a horse can follow a fish. The horse might believe he follows a fish and say he is a fish-follower, but he cannot go where the fish goes, communicate with the fish, or do any fish activities whatsoever. Now what if the horse was remade by a power greater than himself into a fish? Well, then he truly could follow his favorite fish! The Bible makes it clear how a follower is made, and what the life of a follower looks like. So now that you know, let me ask this; Are you one?

Remember:

The gospel is the good news that you can give it all up; give up trying to rescue yourself, give up sin that kills, and give in to a rescuer that will save you from start to finish.[1]

Tech Tip!

If you're wondering if you really are a true Christian, go read the short book of 1st John. We discussed it a bit here, but a careful reading on your own would be a very healthy thing. Don't worry, this little book will be here when you get back!

[1] In Philippians 3:4-13 Paul explains that he's willing to dismiss/forget all his good works, knowing they contribute nothing to salvation.

Have You Met the Grey god?

You may think that the grey god is a facet of modern theology that is found only in the liberal-leaning churches, but I submit to you that this view has crept into almost all modern churches in one form or another, especially in the youth programs.

But I'm getting ahead of myself. Let me first explain what I mean by the expression "grey God." This is the view that God isn't entrenched and immovable in His views and tolerances. It's the idea that the Lord doesn't always see things in black and white, but is tolerant and embraces the in-between. Being in-between black and white on many important issues He is "grey". This view has come about because in these modern times tolerance has been redefined to mean approval and it has become elevated not only to being a virtue, but to being the chief virtue above all others, In fact, our "enlightened" culture is now convinced that the only thing that shouldn't be tolerated is intolerance (disapproval)! Ironic, huh?

For many, it's easy to fall into this trap when discussing Christianity and religion. For example, when a topic such as homosexuality, creation, or the exclusivity of salvation through Christ is brought up, many want to "round out the corners" a little. Instead of boldly proclaiming the true God of the Bible, they introduce a "softer" God. Why? Because they want to make the truths presented in God's Word a little less offensive, a little less pointed.

They feel as the archaic "black and white" God and His "this is right and that is wrong" teachings found in Scripture are just a little too offensive for an "enlightened" society such as the one we now find ourselves.

Folks, let's be clear. The God of the bible is patient, but He is not tolerant. I know of no teachings in Scripture that show the Lord deciding certain sins are semi-okay, or that false teaching is no longer false. He may exercise patience, He may give extended calls to repentance, but never does He change His mind on what is sin and what is righteousness.[1] He does not waver on how men must be saved, or what the judgment toward the unrighteous will be on that final day. Simply put, the Lord of Heaven's Armies is not a tolerant God! To present Him as such is to preach a false message about a fictitious god. The final result is that the unbeliever (often a professing believer who is unknowingly lost) goes away with an even stronger belief in this god they have imagined for themselves, this god who is tolerant of their favorite sins and a casual attitude toward all things holy.

When discussing God the Father, Jesus Christ, salvation, or religion, the true believer must have a backbone. The faithful follower must have a sound and biblical understanding as to what sin truly is and know the character of the holy and perfect God he serves. The evangelist (for that is what all believers are) must be black and white, with no sign of grey except in those few areas our Lord intentionally left without full explanation. Was Elijah grey when he mocked the priests of another religion?[2] How about John the Baptist when he discussed important issues with the Pharisees?[3]

---

[1] Romans 2:4

[2] 1st Kings 18:26-29

[3] Matthew 3:7

Surely Jesus was grey, tolerant and unjudging when confronting those who were simply running a business at the temple, right?[1] The more someone is sanctified, set apart from sin and striving to be holy before their Lord, the more they will become black and white, just like their Master. Great care must be taken to be sure that we are entrenched in the same positions as our black and white God, but once we are, let us never become "grey" to accommodate the comfort of the lost or to avoid discomfort in a conversation. Should we be friendly? Of course! Generous? Yes. Patient? Always. Grey? Never!

[1] John 2:15 see also Matthew 23:23

The End…You made it!

Please come visit the blog sometime by going to:

www.ChurchSalt.com

Or, if you have any feedback or questions, feel free to drop an email to:

Texas.Talkback@gmail.com

You can also follow on Twitter at:

@ChurchSalt

Other Books available by Joe Hamper:

Resetting the Biblical Compass available at OneMillionTracts.com or on Amazon.com

Again, thanks for taking the time to pick me up!

The title of this book, "Unnatural Prayer" doesn't sound al[l] that appealing, does it? In a day and age when we are trying our best to eat whole foods (non GMO, of course), use green energy, and live a holistic lifestyle, the word "unnatural" might sound like something that should be actively avoided. And that's just the problem, most of us are avoiding praying in the way we need to pray, the way our Lord taught us to pray. Why? Because it feels unnatural. True prayer is in alignment with our Lord's desires, puts His will ahead of our own, and this often grates against our sinful nature making it feel "unnatural". In this book, we will take an in-depth look at how our Lord taught us to pray, why it feels unnatural, and how the end result brings more answers, peace and rest in our sovereign God then we ever thought possible.

Joe Hamper is a husband, father, church member, and a Texan. The passion Joe has to help followers of Christ better understand the Bible and the incredible truths it contains is evident in his books and also through his blog on ChurchSalt.com. You can also follow him on Twitter at @ChurchSalt.

Publishers Website:
www.OneMilionTracts.c

Church Salt